A *LifeBuilder* Bible Study

SPIRITUAL GIFTS

8 studies
for individuals or groups
R Paul Stevens

with notes for leaders

D1514031

Getting the Most Out of
Spiritual Gifts

Since the 1960s there has been a groundswell of interest in spiritual gifts. Some of this is associated with the charismatic renewal, the one truly global renewal movement I have witnessed in my own lifetime. I am grateful for this emphasis on the unique giftedness of every person in the family of God for service in the church and the world through the Spirit.

My life work has been to seek in every way possible to liberate the "laity" (the whole people of God) by helping them understand that ministry is not something which "ministers" do exclusively, but instead part of the genetic code of all of God's people. Understanding our spiritual gifts is a critical part of seeing how we are called to participate in ministry and therefore in God's global renewal work.

What Are the Gifts All About?

The problem of examining spiritual gifts in the Bible is twofold. First, to a large extent the "gift" movement has been largely co-opted by the narcissism of Western culture and its preoccupation with personal fulfillment, individualism and selfism. Many popular books on "discovering your spiritual gifts" cave in to this pressure. It is hard for Westerners to grasp the perspective that spiritual gifts are not for *us* but for our service to others, not about finding our identity but rather living out our vocation.

But there is another problem that is closely related to the first. The emphasis of the New Testament is not on something we possess or something given to us at conversion—like an organ transplant—but rather on the work of the Spirit *through* us. This is emphasized by the language used in the New Testament, something we will encounter over and again in our study. Despite frequent suggestions to the contrary, the word usually translated "spiritual gifts"—the Greek word *charisma* (from which we get the English "charismatic")—does not mean "spiritual gift," but rather a "concrete expression of grace." It only refers to "Spirit giftedness" when modified by the adjective *pneummatikon*—"spiritual."* Thus there is good reason to title this study *Spirit Gifts*, but we will go with the more familiar *spiritual gifts*.

The key truth these studies express is this: God the Holy Spirit graciously bestows his own presence and power on ordinary followers of Jesus for loving service to others, for the common good. To explore this truth in study we will consider both discovering spiritual gifts and practicing them. Not all Scripture studied will be from the New Testament, since the work of the Spirit is evident in the saints under the Old Covenant. And the Old Testament provides a broader perspective for ministry in the workplace and for bringing justice to the nations. We need both testaments for a full grasp of what it means to be ministers of the kingdom of God.

Finally, I will suggest that for the discovery and expression of spiritual gifts we need an experimental climate (where people can "try" to serve in new ways beyond their accustomed roles), an environment of openness to the full range of the Spirit's work in the church and world, and brothers and sisters who will affirm what God is doing in and through us by saying things like "In our fellowship God works through you . . ." (and asking others for such feedback). We also need courage to risk making mistakes.** Perhaps the greatest mistake would be to try to contain in any single gift, in any single person, what God has poured out so generously for the common good—God's own empowering presence.

Suggestions for Individual Study

1. As you begin each study, pray that God will speak to you through his Word.

---

*This should usually be capitalized as "Spirit-ual."
**See Paul Stevens, "Equipping for Spiritual Gifts," in George Mallone et al., *Those Controversial Gifts* (Downers Grove, Ill.: InterVarsity Press, 1983), pp. 121-43.

2. Read the introduction to the study and respond to the personal reflection question or exercise. This is designed to help you focus on God and on the theme of the study.

3. Each study deals with a particular passage—so that you can delve into the author's meaning in that context. Read and reread the passage to be studied. The questions are written using the language of the New International Version, so you may wish to use that version of the Bible. The New Revised Standard Version is also recommended.

4. This is an inductive Bible study, designed to help you discover for yourself what Scripture is saying. The study includes three types of questions. *Observation* questions ask about the basic facts: who, what, when, where and how. *Interpretation* questions delve into the meaning of the passage. *Application* questions help you discover the implications of the text for growing in Christ. These three keys unlock the treasures of Scripture.

Write your answers to the questions in the spaces provided or in a personal journal. Writing can bring clarity and deeper understanding of yourself and of God's Word.

5. It might be good to have a Bible dictionary handy. Use it to look up any unfamiliar words, names or places.

6. Use the prayer suggestion to guide you in thanking God for what you have learned and to pray about the applications that have come to mind.

7. You may want to go on to the suggestion under "Now or Later," or you may want to use that idea for your next study.

Suggestions for Members of a Group Study

1. Come to the study prepared. Follow the suggestions for individual study mentioned above. You will find that careful preparation will greatly enrich your time spent in group discussion.

2. Be willing to participate in the discussion. The leader of your group will not be lecturing. Instead, he or she will be encouraging the members of the group to discuss what they have learned. The leader will be asking the questions that are found in this guide.

3. Stick to the topic being discussed. Your answers should be based on the verses which are the focus of the discussion and not on outside authorities such as commentaries or speakers. These studies focus on a particular passage of Scripture. Only rarely should you refer to other portions of the Bible. This allows for everyone to participate in in-depth study on equal ground.

4. Be sensitive to the other members of the group. Listen attentively when they describe what they have learned. You may be surprised by their insights! Each question assumes a variety of answers. Many questions do not have "right" answers, particularly questions that aim at meaning or application. Instead the questions push us to explore the passage more thoroughly.

When possible, link what you say to the comments of others. Also, be affirming whenever you can. This will encourage some of the more hesitant members of the group to participate.

5. Be careful not to dominate the discussion. We are sometimes so eager to express our thoughts that we leave too little opportunity for others to respond. By all means participate! But allow others to also.

6. Expect God to teach you through the passage being discussed and through the other members of the group. Pray that you will have an enjoyable and profitable time together, but also that as a result of the study you will find ways that you can take action individually and/or as a group.

7. Remember that anything said in the group is considered confidential and should not be discussed outside the group unless specific permission is given to do so.

8. If you are the group leader, you will find additional suggestions at the back of the guide.

1

What Are
Spiritual Gifts?

1 Corinthians 12

Everyone in a community has a contribution to make, just as each part of the human body contributes to its ability to function properly. The analogy of the body as a way of understanding how people work interdependently has a long history, dating back even to the ancient Greek and Roman writers, and carrying forward still describes various ways that we work with others today.

GROUP DISCUSSION. Describe how the members of a nonchurch organization (a business, club, school or team) you have joined functioned in relation to one another. How did the different abilities of the members contribute (or not contribute) to the purpose of the whole?

PERSONAL REFLECTION. What fears and what longings does the term "spiritual gifts" bring to your mind?

Paul says to the Corinthians that the church is not "like a body" but rather *is* the body of Christ, and individually they are members of that body (1 Corinthians 12:27). Through the Spirit each person has a vital contribution to make to the whole. In 1 Corinthians 12, Paul calls these contributions "spiritual gifts" (v. 1), "gifts" (v. 3) and "manifestation[s] of the Spirit" (v. 7). *Read 1 Corinthians 12:1-13.*

1. What do these verses tell you about how you would know that something that is said to be from God is really genuine (vv. 1-3)?

If you know them • *If it does not contradict scipture*
* *It doesn't have to make Sense*   Get Someo
* *These verses do not contain enough detail*   To Confir
                                                  or

2. What is your personal response to the statement that "each one" is *Have a*
given a manifestation of the Spirit (v. 7)?   *Eldersh*

Everyone has been gifted

Everyone can Serve.

3. *Read 1 Corinthians 12:14-31.* Paul's concern is not just unity but diversity in the family of God. Trace the argument Paul uses in the previous section and this one to emphasize the need for many diverse expressions of the Spirit in the life of the church.

* *Emphasises Unit "but still there is only one body" V.2*
* *Different Treatment V. 24*   +
* *"Each one Separate + necessary part of it" V.27*   V.2

4. The Corinthians apparently put the highest priority on one or two gifts. How would the church look if all the members had the same gift or if they prized one gift over all the others?

5. In what way is Paul's argument a solution for our personal feelings of inferiority or superiority in the body of Christ (vv. 22-26)?

We are all ... necessary   V.27

6. Describe in your own words how each one of the gifts Paul lists here might be manifested (vv. 8-11, 28-30). *Alex*
Alex
Alex
Alex

Although Paul does not intend this to be a complete list of gifts, which of these have you seen at work in your own church, fellowship or small group?

Romans 12 v 6-8   Eph 4 v 11-13

7. How in your own experience has exercising spiritual gifts served "the common good" (v. 7) and prevented (rather than caused) "discord in the body" (v. 25)? *Peacemakers ?.*

Teachers ?.

What attitudes and actions would lead to disunity and schism?

False Teachers

8. What comfort do you gain from knowing that it is God who gives the gifts (v. 11) and who "combines the members" of the body (v. 24)? *He is directing. Our church will have what/who it needs, when it needs it.*

9. What have you learned about the character and the purpose of spiritual gifts?

10. What challenge do you have from the exhortation to "desire the greater gifts" (v. 31)? *We should be pestering God for them*

Ask God to show you how to serve others in the body even if you cannot "name" the spiritual gift he has given you.

Now or Later

Study the headship of Jesus in the body in the following Scriptures: Acts 4:11; Ephesians 5:23; Colossians 1:18; 1 Peter 2:7. Then study how Jesus apportions the gifts through the Spirit according to his own purposes: Acts 2:4; 3:16; 11:17; 1 Corinthians 3:5; 12:7-8, 24; Ephesians 3:2, 8; 4:7-8, 11; 1 Peter 4:10.

2

Equipping the Saints for Ministry

Ephesians 4:1-16

Often when we walk into a church, we are aware that there are two types of people—one called "clergy" and the other called "laity." They dress differently, talk differently, work differently and sometimes even think differently. One gives ministry. The other receives ministry. Yet when we "walk into" the New Testament we meet not two groups of people separated by titles, education and roles, but one people (called the "people of God" in the original Greek) with leaders among them, referred to in Scripture by terms that describe their different functions in the church.

GROUP DISCUSSION. What do you think is the reason people in the church are often content with the status quo, with being consumers of good sermons and spine-tingling worship rather than entering into the full inheritance of the people of God?

PERSONAL REFLECTION. Review the contexts in which you have given or received ministry. Who were the people? What was the context or culture? What encouragement or discouragement did you experience in giving or receiving ministry?

Paul's letter to the Ephesians divides into two parts. Chapters 1-3 describe our incredible identity in Christ: chosen, redeemed, sealed in the Spirit and incorporated into Christ's body. Then in 4:1 Paul begins to address the calling or vocation that comes to the body as a whole and to each believer individually. All (and not just pastors and missionaries) are summoned to walk worthy of that calling. Paul spells out how this works out in the church (chapter 4), the home (chapter 5 and part of chapter 6) and the world (chapter 6). *Read Ephesians 4:1-16.*

1. What is Paul's main concern for the church as they "walk worthy of their calling"?

What would Paul regard as evidence that they had walked worthy?

Where and when, if ever, have you experienced this in your own community life?

2. What is the source and nature of the unity that the church starts with and must maintain (v. 3), and what is the unity that must be attained (v. 13)?

3. In this passage Paul shows how the giving of spiritual gifts is the result of Christ's coming as a human being, his saving work through "descending" on the cross, his ascension into heaven and the outpouring of himself through (it is implied) the Spirit (vv. 8-11). What difference does this make in regard to how many of the people of God might be ministers?

4. How do you respond to the truth that you are a fraction of the image of Christ, a person who has a portion of Christ's grace flowing through you (v. 7)?

5. What is the purpose of those leaders in the church who bring the Word of God (vv. 11-12)?

6. Commonly it is thought that the pastor's job is to deliver the ministry, and the work of the rest of the people is to assist her or him. What change in the life of your church would take place if pastors were called to assist the rest of the people in *their* ministry?

7. What do verses 2, 14-16 tell us about the relational dimensions of equipping the saints in their "calling"?

8. Most people think that the purpose of spiritual gifts is exclusively to fill the church (through worship, healing, teaching and encouragement). What could it mean to "fill the whole universe" (v. 10)?

Give some positive examples in your town, city, university or workplace where such spiritual gift ministry might bring in the presence of Christ's kingdom beyond the church gathered for worship.

9. What kind of church growth results from equipping spiritual gifts (vv. 12-16)?

10. Neither overworked pastors nor underemployed "laypersons" can liberate themselves. What positive steps can be taken in your church to facilitate a mutual liberation and so release the pastor from an impossible role and the rest from mere "busy" work?

In humility thank the Lord for choosing you to be a servant/minister for him in the church and the world. Ask him to keep you from self-despising and arrogance, that you may truly be an agent of blessing to others.

Now or Later

Study the various uses of the word *equip* (sometimes translated "restore," "prepare," "train" or "complete") in the New Testament and how these might illuminate the various ways people can be equipped for using their spiritual gifts. For example, consider different models of equipping the saints in the Bible: (1) discipleship (Paul mentoring Timothy); (2) shared teaching (Paul and Barnabas leading a Bible study in Antioch together for a year); (3) public teaching with dialogue and interaction at the Hall of Tyrannus (Acts 19:9-10); (4) life-on-life equipping (Jesus and the Twelve).

For further reading on the ministry of the whole people of God, check out Greg Ogden, *The New Reformation*; Sue Mallory, *The Equipping Church*; or R. Paul Stevens and Phil Collins, *The Equipping Pastor.*

3

Discovering
Spiritual Gifts

Romans 12:1-13
1 Thessalonians 5:19-22

Forrest Gump says that life is like a box of chocolates. You never quite know what you are going to get when you open it.

GROUP DISCUSSION. Have each person finish the following sentence: "The most surprising and unexpected thing I have discovered about myself since emerging into adulthood is . . ."

PERSONAL REFLECTION. Consider what brought you joy and what you felt was fruitful in helping others in various periods of your life: ages 1-11, 12-16, 17-25, 26-35, 36-50 and so on. Is there a common thread in terms of the kind of activity, the materials you worked with and the way you related to people?

Spiritual gifts are not add-ons to our lives, like spiritual organ transplants. They are the empowerings of the Spirit through the whole person God has created. Thus we are not likely to discover these gifts if we do not know ourselves. Chapter 12 in Paul's letter to the Romans has much to say on this double knowing. *Read Romans 12:1-13.*

---

1. Summarize in one sentence what Paul says about our relationship with (1) God (v. 1), (2) the world (v. 2), (3) ourselves (v. 3), (4) our brothers and sisters in the family of God (vv. 4-8), and (5) our neighbors near and far (vv. 9-13).

Which of these statements do you find personally most challenging? Why?

2. Why do you think the presentation of our whole bodily life (and not just our "spiritual" activities) pleases God and is our sensible worship (v. 1)?

3. While many people suffer from too low a view of themselves, how would too high a self-concept especially frustrate the outworking of spiritual gifts in community life (vv. 4-6)?

4. Paul notes the wonderful diversity in the body of Christ at the same time as he emphasizes that "each member belongs to all the others" (v. 5). How does this unity that is "because of" diversity help you to relate to people who have different gifts than yours or whose gifts you might covet?

5. People who are not yet Christians also serve, teach, encourage, give, lead and show mercy. What extra benefits do verses 6-8 refer to in regard to the work of the Spirit as we use these gifts?

6. First Timothy 4:14 says, "Do not neglect your gift, which was given you through a prophetic message when the body of elders laid their hands on you." What further can we learn about discovering and nurturing spiritual gifts from Timothy's experience?

7. *Read 1 Thessalonians 5:19-22.* Describe how you might test the spiritual gifts of others, or your own.

8. What is the role of self-examination and of affirmation from others in discovering spiritual gifts?

9. Consider whether you think it is important to be able to "name" your spiritual gift. What dangers are there in this?

10. What can you now say to someone who feels that they don't know what their gift is?

Pray that through God's mercy and the Spirit's continued work in your life you will be inspired to serve your brothers and sisters with grace and power. Ask God to keep you from being squeezed into the world's mold.

Now or Later

Examine more carefully the ministry of believers to near and far neighbors and to enemies in Romans 12:9-21. Without calling these functions "gifts" or even "ministries," Paul counsels a radical way of living by love. John Stott says that "*philadelphia* (love of sisters and brothers) has to be balanced by *philozenia* (love of the stranger)."* Read the story of Abraham and Sarah's pursuit of the stranger in Genesis 18:1-15 and the New Testament exhortation in Hebrews 13:2 based on this Old Testament story.

*John Stott, *The Message of Romans* (Downers Grove, Ill.: InterVarsity Press, 2001), p. 332.

4

Those Controversial Gifts

I Corinthians 14:1-33

We each have different comfort levels in situations we cannot control or when people say things that are completely unexpected. But we all experience discomfort during a family feud, an unexpected interruption during a church service or a business meeting that turns sour. At the same time, in each of these settings we may also experience comfort, encouragement, instruction and sometimes even healing.

GROUP DISCUSSION. At this point in the studies you may be beginning to sense the particular way that each person is contributing and serving. Without naming a gift mentioned in Paul's lists, and without identifying the person, use a single word or a short phrase to describe some of the manifestations of the Spirit that you have experienced in the group. Examples could be "clarifying a difficult thought," "making me feel welcome," "affirming," "praying right into my heart," "making Scripture clear."

PERSONAL REFLECTION. Recall a situation when something happened outside of your "comfort zone." What were your feelings? How did you react? What were you thinking?

Most of us feel safe with gifts such as teaching, helps, leadership, evangelism and giving aid to others. But what can we do about those spontaneous, unplanned expressions of Spirit life that sometimes interrupt our order of service, or never take place because we want to keep the lid on everything that happens when we are together? Are they partly, or mostly, from "the flesh"? Did they die out with the first century now that we have the written Scripture? Or are they needful and truly wonderful contributions to the upbuilding of people in Christ? Having dealt with the need for diversity (1 Corinthians 12) and the critical role of love in motivating spiritual gifts (1 Corinthians 13), Paul takes up the point he ended with in chapter 12. *Read 1 Corinthians 14:1-12.*

1. What does Paul have to say in this passage about why we should "eagerly desire the greater gifts" (12:31)?

2. What abuse in spiritual gift expression is Paul seeking to correct (v. 12)?

3. What is your greatest hope or your greatest fear when you consider the spontaneous and supernatural expressions of Spirit-ministry in the life of your group or church?

4. In your own words, describe how Paul argues from everyday life that tongues (speaking in unknown languages in prayer) without interpretation is useless in a community situation (vv. 7-11).

5. What is required for a revelation, a word of knowledge, a prophecy or a teaching to benefit others (v. 6)?

6. *Read 1 Corinthians 14:13-33.* Until now Paul has been arguing for the benefit supernatural utterances can bring, under certain conditions, to believers when they are together. How, in contrast, might they hinder an unbeliever who comes into the fellowship?

How might they help?

7. What indication is there that these supernatural gifts are under the control of the speaker and not, as in pagan religious ecstasies, a mindless and uncontrollable state (vv. 30-31)?

8. From verse 26, what picture do you get of worship services in the first century?

How is this different from and similar to your own experience of believers gathering together?

9. On what basis does Paul appeal for order in the church?

How could some approaches to keeping everything "decent and in order" actually prevent spontaneous Spirit ministry and thereby quench the Spirit?

Ask the Lord to help you deal with your fears about situations you can't control. Pray that the Lord will empower you to trust him more and be open to new ways he might minister to you and through you.

Now or Later

Study the gift of prophecy in Scripture.

The classical definition of a prophet in the Old Testament is one who speaks for God in foretelling the future or telling forth God's view of a situation. Moses is an example, predicting the release of the captives (Exodus 3:15-22) and announcing the moral imperatives the people should follow (Exodus 19:1-6).

In the New Testament the outpouring of the Holy Spirit made everyone potentially a prophet (Acts 2:17-18), thus fulfilling Moses' prayer (Numbers 11:29) and Jeremiah's prophecy (Jeremiah 31:31-34). While some New Testament prophets foretold the future (Acts 11:27-30), normally prophecy was "speaking forth."

All prophecy must be tested from Scripture (2 Timothy 3:16-17; 1 Corinthians 14:37-38) according to whether the lordship and ministry of Christ is confessed (1 Corinthians 12:1-3), thus questioning words that are pure and unadulterated judgment, lacking in grace, and according to the character of the person speaking (Matthew 7:15-20; Galatians 5:22-23).

5

Spiritual Gifts
for Liberation

> ## Isaiah 61:1-9;
> ## Luke 4:14-21

In the Western world salvation, faith and spirituality have become largely a private matter. During Old Testament times, however, it was unthinkable to separate knowing God from seeking social justice, correcting oppression, and caring for the poor and marginalized. The situation in the world today is marked by huge inequalities between the rich and the poor (and the gap is getting wider), with millions dying of hunger and global resources being consumed disproportionately by a fraction of the world's population.

GROUP DISCUSSION. Consider the smaller "world" of your city, town or university. What issues seem most unjust to you and make you want to make something right—if only you could?

PERSONAL REFLECTION. Review some of the influences in your own life from your childhood to the present. What experiences, people and groups have caused you to look beyond yourself to people struggling with hopeless neediness or unfair treatment by those in power?

In his magnificent book of prophecy the prophet Isaiah both tells forth (speaking God's word with immediacy to actual situations in the eighth century B.C.) and foretells (speaking about future events, especially the coming of the Messiah). The central future prophecy in the book is about the Messiah (or "Christ") who will be the anointed Savior. This great God-man deliverer is sometimes pictured as a king, sometimes as a suffering servant and, in this passage, as an anointed conqueror. *Read Isaiah 61:1-3.*

---

1. What does the anointed conqueror say about himself in his relationship to God?

---

2. This wonderful person not only is God's man but does God's work. Describe the people he is sent to.

---

3. Think of your own city and country. Who would be the people most likely to hear this message as "good news"?

---

4. In what ways is this message different from or the same as the preaching you have heard in your lifetime?

---

5. Why would the anointing of the Spirit be so important to accomplish this mission?

6. *Read Luke 4:14-21.* Jesus quoted this text in his first sermon in his hometown synagogue of Nazareth, claiming he fulfilled it in his own person. Why do you think Jesus stopped short of saying he had come to proclaim "the day of vengeance of our God" (Isaiah 61:2)?

7. Why do you think bringing good news to the poor is so central to authentic biblical Christianity?

How could you use your spiritual gifts to bring good news to the poor?

8. In Isaiah 61:1-3 the prophet has announced the effect the anointed deliverer (Christ) will have on individual people. *Read Isaiah 61:4-9.* What effects will the Messiah have on a devastated creation and on the devastated people as a whole?

9. What are the signs that God's kingdom has actually come?

10. What evidence is there that not only the chosen people but all nations will be blessed because of the work of the Messiah?

11. All of this gracious work of transformation is through the mediation of the blessings of the Holy Spirit by the Messiah. What have you learned from this study about being "priests" and "ministers" of the Lord (61:6) in the power and presence of the Spirit and Word?

In your own situation, what can you do to share in God's work of righteousness (making things right)?

Ask the Lord to equip you to share in his great work of making things right in the world.

Now or Later

Consider other prophecies in the Bible about the coming of the Anointed Conqueror who would also be the Suffering Servant: Genesis 3:15; 22:18; 49:10; Deuteronomy 18:15; Psalm 2:7; 16:10; 45:2; 68:18; 69:21; 110:1; 118:22; 132:11; Isaiah 7:14; 9:6; 11:1; 28:16; 42:1; 52:13—53:12; 59:16; 61:1; 63:1; Jeremiah 23:5; Daniel 9:25; Micah 5:2; Haggai 2:7; Zechariah 3:8; 6:12; 9:9; 11:12; 12:10; 13:7; Malachi 3:1.

Research the Scriptures that emphasize God's compassion for the poor and his anger toward the mighty and strong oppressors in the world: Exodus 2:23-24; Isaiah 1:17; 3:14-15; 10:1-2; Job 24; Amos 2:6-8; 4:1-3; 6:1-7; Micah 2:1-2; 6:6-16.

6

Spiritual Gifts in Relationships

Galatians 5:16-26

We live in tension as we look at the evil others inflict. We see the tyranny of racism and the possibility that terrorists will strike again. But the most troubling tension is within ourselves as we relate to others: predatory competitiveness, possessiveness, envy and jealousy, and sexual lust.

GROUP DISCUSSION. Consider the following list of what goes wrong in our relationships. Which one most troubles you? Why?

- *Sexual impurity:* pornography, adultery, homosexuality, sexual innuendos
- *Idolatry:* making something or someone your ultimate concern other than the One who is ultimate, such as money, material things, work, ministry, family, body, popularity, power, entertainment
- *Occult:* fortunes, séances, astrology, witchcraft, superstitions
- *Relational sin:* bitterness, resentment, unforgiveness, jealousy, violent thoughts and acts, cruelty in word or deed, backbiting, quarreling, stealing, ridiculing, impatience, gossip, hatred, lying
- *Attitudes:* anger, envy, anxiety, fear, selfish ambition, arrogance, self-righteousness, insecurity, self-hatred, greed, covetousness, laziness

PERSONAL REFLECTION. Reflect silently on the most difficult relationship you have had. Without naming the person involved, describe what you understand to be your part in this troubling experience.

We have been looking at spiritual gifts as specific, gracious bestowments of God for service in the church and world. But now we turn to a complementary subject that is critical for expressing spiritual gifts: the fruit of the Spirit. In Galatians Paul outlines how the Spirit works in us as we start the Christian life (3:3) and continue in that life. He calls the Galatians back to the gospel and away from the religion of works and performance they were slipping into. *Read Galatians 5:16-21.*

---

1. In this passage Paul uses "the sinful nature," sometimes translated "flesh," to describe human nature as a whole, not just our bodies. It is human nature as it has become through sin, turned in on itself and lived outside of God's empowering presence. Describe in your own words the tension Paul identifies in verses 16-18.

---

2. Which of the "works of the sinful nature [flesh]" are most evident in your workplace, your society, your church and your own home?

---

3. Why is it important for you to identify the exact nature of the tension and conflict that you daily experience, and not just cover it up?

---

4. Why do you think we still have conflict, perhaps even more than before becoming a Christian, when Christ has accomplished our salvation and the Spirit is at work in our lives?

5. What does this passage say to those who "live like this" (5:21), making the works of the sinful nature a habitual way of life?

---

6. *Read Galatians 5:22-26.* Spiritual gifts are described in plural form, while Paul uses the singular form in talking about the Spirit's work in relationships: the ninefold *fruit* of the Spirit. Which dimensions of the "fruit" concern our relationship with God?

our relationship with others?

our relationship to our self?

---

7. Describe how the fruit actually works in relationships within the church and in the work world.

---

8. Why does it mean, in practical terms, that there is no law against these (v. 23)?

9. What solution does Paul offer for the ongoing battle between flesh and spirit?

How is our strategy in this battle both relying on the Spirit's work and taking active disciplinary steps ourselves (vv. 16, 24-25)? Why would one without the other spell disaster?

---

10. What have you learned about the importance of Spirit-fruit when expressing spiritual gifts in the church and world?

Ask the Lord to keep you from being a "fruit inspector" in others. Pray that he would reveal his image through your character and actions.

Now or Later

Paul's fruit of the Spirit is throughout Scripture: love (Romans 13:8-10; 1 Corinthians 13:1-13; 16:14; Ephesians 5:21; Colossians 3:14; 1 Thessalonians 3:12; 4:9-10); joy (Romans 14:17; 15:13; 1 Thessalonians 5:16); peace (Romans 14:1—15:30; 16:20; Ephesians 2:14-17; 2 Thessalonians 3:16); forbearance (1 Corinthians 13:4; Colossians 3:12); kindness (Romans 2:4; 3:12; 11:22; 2 Corinthians 6:6; Galatians 5:22; Ephesians 2:7; Colossians 3:12; Titus 3:4); goodness (Romans 15:14); faithfulness (Romans 3:3); gentleness (Matthew 11:25-30; 1 Corinthians 4:21; 2 Corinthians 10:1; Galatians 5:23; 6:1; Ephesians 4:2; Colossians 3:12; 1 Timothy 6:11; 2 Timothy 2:25; Titus 3:2); self-control (1 Corinthians 10:31-33; 14:1-23; Colossians 2:16-23; 1 Timothy 4:1-5). Read and reflect on these texts.

7

Spiritual Gifts in the Workplace

*Exodus 31:1-11;
35:4-19; 35:30—36:7*

Many believers feel motivated to serve God wholeheartedly in church services and religious activities but lack passion about their daily work in the world. At the same time, ours is a work-oriented society. But so often work promises to contribute more to our lives than it can deliver—meaning, personal fulfillment and the use of our talents to the maximum. Studs Terkel, interviewing people about their work life, found that for many it was a "daily humiliation."*

GROUP DISCUSSION. Describe your most dissatisfying work experience (whether in remunerated work or as a volunteer) and what made it so frustrating. Then describe your most meaningful work experience and what made it purposeful.

PERSONAL REFLECTION. Review your work life from your earliest memories as a child, covering the major periods of your life (childhood, youth, early adulthood, adulthood). What did you enjoy doing, and what did you feel you did successfully? Where do you think God might have been in all this?

The Old Testament book of Exodus contains a fascinating vignette of two craftspeople—Bezalel and his assistant, Oholiab. They are remembered in the context of their work in building the tent of meeting for the people of God. The people of Israel had been rescued from slavery in Egypt, had been given a covenant and law at Mount Sinai, and now were instructed to build a tent meeting place for God to dwell with the people continuously. Bezalel and Oholiab give us a fascinating and important perspective on the Spirit's gifts for work in the world. Bezalel is the only person in the Old Testament of whom it is said he was "filled with the Spirit of God." *Read Exodus 31:1-11.*

---

1. What manifestations of the Spirit were evident in Bezalel's life? (Note the range of materials and the range of worship articles that Bezalel and his assistant were skilled in working with.)

---

2. What special gift does Oholiab bring to the task of building the Tent?

---

3. Why do you think it might be important to have a Spirit-gift for work (even so-called secular work) and not just Spirit infilling for worship services or pastoral ministry?

---

4. Chapter 35 restates the process of building the tent after Israel committed the terrible sin of idolatry and Moses interceded on their behalf. *Read Exodus 35:4-19.* How do all the people contribute to building the meeting place with God?

5. *Read Exodus 35:30—36:7.* What further endowment does God give both Bezalel and Oholiab (35:34)?

Why is this gift important for the work that needs to be done?

---

6. What important clue do we learn about the Spirit's gifting for our work life from the two leading craftsmen and others involved in the project (36:2)?

---

7. In the case of the workers in this story there were three dimensions in discerning giftedness: divine initiative (called by name, 31:2); heart desire (willing to do the work, 36:2); recognition by the community (Moses identified the workers and commissioned them, 36:2). Why would all three be important to your own vocational discernment?

---

8. While Bezalel is the only person in the Old Testament actually described as "filled with the Spirit," many others received the Spirit in various manners for special services. But before Christ the Spirit's gift was temporary, occasional and selective. Under the new covenant in Christ, the Holy Spirit's presence is permanent, continuous and universal. Why do you think so many Christians function in the church and world as though we were still under the older covenant?

What difference does it make to you to know that the Spirit empowers all believers for serving God and neighbor?

9. What have you learned from the example of Bezalel and Oholiab that can be applied to your life in the work world?

Ask God to fill you with his Spirit that you may work in the world with wisdom, discernment and ability.

Now or Later

Research the ways that God leads people into Spirit-empowered work in the world in the Old Testament: Joseph (Genesis 37—41), Nehemiah (Nehemiah 2), Esther (Esther 1—2), Daniel (Daniel 1). In the New Testament, study the teaching concerning working for God and neighbor (Acts 20:32-35; Ephesians 4:28; 6:5-9; Colossians 3:22—4:1; 2 Thessalonians 3:6-10; 1 Timothy 5:8; 6:1-25).

---

*Quoted in Joanne B. Ciulla, *The Working Life: The Promise and Betrayal of Modern Work* (New York: Three Rivers Press, 2000), p. xiv.

8

Spiritual Gifts
in Witness

Acts 2:1-21, 37-47

Witnessing is hard, especially in a postmodern, post-Christian society. Most people outside the church think they have heard the Christian message even though they have really opted for some other spirituality or some form of humanistic self-realization. So the response of the church is often to become an ingrown gathering, growing itself rather than bringing in the kingdom of God.

GROUP DISCUSSION. The church is both a gathering (on Sunday) and a spreading out (on Monday). Determine where God has sovereignly placed fifteen or twenty members of your church, including members of your own study group, on Monday morning. What would mission look like if every member were a missionary right where they are? How could the Sunday gathering serve to empower people for Monday mission?

PERSONAL REFLECTION. Where have you been in the last seven days? Consider the places you have been, the people you have met, the situations you have encountered.

In contrast to the self-preoccupation of much of the Western church, the early church was "on the go," a sent people on a mission for God. The risen Christ had promised his people that they would be "clothed with power from on high" (Luke 24:49) to empower them for their mission. During this celebration of the day of Pentecost, a Jewish feast commemorating the day the Law was given (Genesis 10), the promised Holy Spirit arrives. *Read Acts 2:1-13.*

1. Describe what the gathered believers hear, see and witness on this day.

2. What is the effect on the international gathering of the Holy Spirit's outpouring on the believers?

What temporary conclusion do some draw?

What explanation does Peter give?

3. When, if ever, have you thought that a spiritual manifestation was a matter of intoxication, either chemical or emotional?

What would have convinced you that the manifestation was a genuine Spirit-gift?

4. Peter, quoting the Old Testament prophet Joel, claims that the "last days" are here, beginning with the death, resurrection and ascension of Jesus, and the outpouring of the Holy Spirit. What difference does it make for the first generation of Christians to know that they are in the "last days"?

What difference does it make for us, many centuries after the day of Pentecost?

5. Which spiritual gifts are especially associated with these "last days" (vv. 17-18)?

Who receives these gifts?

6. After quoting Joel, Peter promises that whomever turns to the Lord will be saved (v. 21). He preaches a sermon that tells the story of Jesus (vv. 22-36). *Read Acts 2:37-47.* What is the response of the people?

What is the scope of "what my Father has promised" (Luke 24:49) and "the promise" (Acts 2:39; see also 1:4, 8)?

7. What do we learn from this critical incident about the ministry of evangelism?

---

8. What have you learned from this study about the role of spiritual gifts in witnessing?

---

9. Describe the community that is so greatly enlarged on this day. Consider their common life, their experience of spiritual gifts, their worship, their relation to the apostles and the apostles' teaching, and their outreach.

---

10. What are some of the main things you have learned from all eight studies about the purpose and place of spiritual gifts?

Ask God to empower you to open your heart and mouth, as you have opportunity, to put in a good word for Jesus.

Now or Later

Study some further Spirit-empowered witness in the first days of the church:
- Peter and John's healing of the man by the Beautiful Gate (Acts 3:1-10)
- Peter's sermon and explanation of the miracle (3:11-28)
- Peter's testimony after being put in custody and many more believing (4:1-4)

- Peter's being filled with the Holy Spirit (4:8) and preaching to the Jewish leaders (4:5-22)
- the extraordinary prayer of the believers leading to speaking the word of God with boldness (4:23-31)
- the fellowship (4:32-37)
- signs and wonders being performed by the apostles (5:12-16)
- the apostles imprisoned and miraculously released (5:17-42), at which time they immediately go on witnessing (5:25, 42)
- the persecution and scattering of the believers after Stephen's martyrdom, witnessing wherever they went (8:1-4)
- Philip going to Samaria, confronting a magician and preaching good news about the kingdom of God and the name of Jesus Christ (8:5-13)
- the Samaritans receiving the Holy Spirit (8:14-25)
- Philip being led by the Spirit to a traveling inquirer from Ethiopia, leading him to Christ and baptizing him (8:26-40)
- Cornelius, a Gentile, spoken to by an angel of God at the same time as Peter is given a vision leading him to a meeting where the Holy Spirit is poured out on the Gentiles present and they speak in tongues (10:1-48)

As each frontier is crossed (the Samaritans, then proselytes and finally the Gentiles), there are manifestations of the Holy Spirit. God is previous in the witness, present in the witness, and confirming and sealing people into God's family.

Leader's Notes

MY GRACE IS SUFFICIENT FOR YOU. (2 COR 12:9)

Leading a Bible discussion can be an enjoyable and rewarding experience. But it can also be *scary*—especially if you've never done it before. If this is your feeling, you're in good company. When God asked Moses to lead the Israelites out of Egypt, he replied, "O LORD, please send someone else to do it" (Ex 4:13). It was the same with Solomon, Jeremiah and Timothy, but God helped these people in spite of their weaknesses, and he will help you as well.

You don't need to be an expert on the Bible or a trained teacher to lead a Bible discussion. The idea behind these inductive studies is that the leader guides group members to discover for themselves what the Bible has to say. This method of learning will allow group members to remember much more of what is said than a lecture would.

These studies are designed to be led easily. As a matter of fact, the flow of questions through the passage from observation to interpretation to application is so natural that you may feel that the studies lead themselves. This study guide is also flexible. You can use it with a variety of groups—student, professional, neighborhood or church groups. Each study takes forty-five to sixty minutes in a group setting.

There are some important facts to know about group dynamics and encouraging discussion. The suggestions listed below should enable you to effectively and enjoyably fulfill your role as leader.

Preparing for the Study

1. Ask God to help you understand and apply the passage in your own life. Unless this happens, you will not be prepared to lead others. Pray too for the various members of the group. Ask God to open your hearts to the message of his Word and motivate you to action.

2. Read the introduction to the entire guide to get an overview of the entire book and the issues which will be explored.

3. As you begin each study, read and reread the assigned Bible passage to familiarize yourself with it.

4. This study guide is based on the New International Version of the Bible. It will help you and the group if you use this translation as the basis for your study and discussion.

5. Carefully work through each question in the study. Spend time in meditation and reflection as you consider how to respond.

6. Write your thoughts and responses in the space provided in the study guide. This will help you to express your understanding of the passage clearly.

7. It might help to have a Bible dictionary handy. Use it to look up any unfamiliar words, names or places. (For additional help on how to study a passage, see chapter five of *How to Lead a LifeGuide Bible Study,* InterVarsity Press.)

8. Consider how you can apply the Scripture to your life. Remember that the group will follow your lead in responding to the studies. They will not go any deeper than you do.

9. Once you have finished your own study of the passage, familiarize yourself with the leader's notes for the study you are leading. These are designed to help you in several ways. First, they tell you the purpose the study guide author had in mind when writing the study. Take time to think through how the study questions work together to accomplish that purpose. Second, the notes provide you with additional background information or suggestions on group dynamics for various questions. This information can be useful when people have difficulty understanding or answering a question. Third, the leader's notes can alert you to potential problems you may encounter during the study.

10. If you wish to remind yourself of anything mentioned in the leader's notes, make a note to yourself below that question in the study.

Leading the Study

1. Begin the study on time. Open with prayer, asking God to help the group to understand and apply the passage.

2. Be sure that everyone in your group has a study guide. Encourage the group to prepare beforehand for each discussion by reading the introduction to the guide and by working through the questions in the study.

3. At the beginning of your first time together, explain that these studies are meant to be discussions, not lectures. Encourage the members of the group to participate. However, do not put pressure on those who may be hesitant to speak during the first few sessions. You may want to suggest the following guidelines to your group.

☐ Stick to the topic being discussed.

☐ Your responses should be based on the verses which are the focus of the discussion and not on outside authorities such as commentaries or speakers.

☐ These studies focus on a particular passage of Scripture. Only rarely should you refer to other portions of the Bible. This allows for everyone to participate in in-depth study on equal ground.

☐ Anything said in the group is considered confidential and will not be discussed outside the group unless specific permission is given to do so.

☐ We will listen attentively to each other and provide time for each person present to talk.

☐ We will pray for each other.

4. Have a group member read the introduction at the beginning of the discussion.

5. Every session begins with a group discussion question. The question or activity is meant to be used before the passage is read. The question introduces the theme of the study and encourages group members to begin to open up. Encourage as many members as possible to participate, and be ready to get the discussion going with your own response.

This section is designed to reveal where our thoughts or feelings need to be transformed by Scripture. That is why it is especially important not to read the passage before the discussion question is asked. The passage will tend to color the honest reactions people would otherwise give because they are, of course, supposed to think the way the Bible does.

You may want to supplement the group discussion question with an icebreaker to help people to get comfortable. See the community section of *Small Group Idea Book* for more ideas.

You also might want to use the personal reflection question with your group. Either allow a time of silence for people to respond individually or discuss it together.

6. Have a group member (or members if the passage is long) read aloud the passage to be studied. Then give people several minutes to read the passage again silently so that they can take it all in.

7. Question 1 will generally be an overview question designed to briefly survey the passage. Encourage the group to look at the whole passage, but try to avoid getting sidetracked by questions or issues that will be addressed later in the study.

8. As you ask the questions, keep in mind that they are designed to be used just as they are written. You may simply read them aloud. Or you may prefer to express them in your own words.

There may be times when it is appropriate to deviate from the study guide.

For example, a question may have already been answered. If so, move on to the next question. Or someone may raise an important question not covered in the guide. Take time to discuss it, but try to keep the group from going off on tangents.

9. Avoid answering your own questions. If necessary, repeat or rephrase them until they are clearly understood. Or point out something you read in the leader's notes to clarify the context or meaning. An eager group quickly becomes passive and silent if they think the leader will do most of the talking.

10. Don't be afraid of silence. People may need time to think about the question before formulating their answers.

11. Don't be content with just one answer. Ask, "What do the rest of you think?" or "Anything else?" until several people have given answers to the question.

12. Acknowledge all contributions. Try to be affirming whenever possible. Never reject an answer. If it is clearly off-base, ask, "Which verse led you to that conclusion?" or again, "What do the rest of you think?"

13. Don't expect every answer to be addressed to you, even though this will probably happen at first. As group members become more at ease, they will begin to truly interact with each other. This is one sign of healthy discussion.

14. Don't be afraid of controversy. It can be very stimulating. If you don't resolve an issue completely, don't be frustrated. Move on and keep it in mind for later. A subsequent study may solve the problem.

15. Periodically summarize what the group has said about the passage. This helps to draw together the various ideas mentioned and gives continuity to the study. But don't preach.

16. At the end of the Bible discussion you may want to allow group members a time of quiet to work on an idea under "Now or Later." Then discuss what you experienced. Or you may want to encourage group members to work on these ideas between meetings. Give an opportunity during the session for people to talk about what they are learning.

17. Conclude your time together with conversational prayer, adapting the prayer suggestion at the end of the study to your group. Ask for God's help in following through on the commitments you've made.

18. End on time.

Many more suggestions and helps are found in *How to Lead a LifeGuide Bible Study.*

Components of Small Groups
A healthy small group should do more than study the Bible. There are four

components to consider as you structure your time together.

Nurture. Small groups help us to grow in our knowledge and love of God. Bible study is the key to making this happen and is the foundation of your small group.

Community. Small groups are a great place to develop deep friendships with other Christians. Allow time for informal interaction before and after each study. Plan activities and games that will help you get to know each other. Spend time having fun together—going on a picnic or cooking dinner together.

Worship and prayer. Your study will be enhanced by spending time praising God together in prayer or song. Pray for each other's needs—and keep track of how God is answering prayer in your group. Ask God to help you to apply what you are learning in your study.

Outreach. Reaching out to others can be a practical way of applying what you are learning, and it will keep your group from becoming self-focused. Host a series of evangelistic discussions for your friends or neighbors. Clean up the yard of an elderly friend. Serve at a soup kitchen together, or spend a day working on a Habitat house.

Many more suggestions and helps in each of these areas are found in *Small Group Idea Book.* Information on building a small group can be found in *Small Group Leaders' Handbook* and *The Big Book on Small Groups* (both from Inter-Varsity Press). Reading through one of these books would be worth your time.

Study 1. What Are Spiritual Gifts? 1 Corinthians 12

Purpose: To discover the source and purpose of spiritual gifts in the people of God.

General note. According to Gordon Fee, Paul has been dealing with matters of worship since 1 Corinthians 8, and the issue at question for the Corinthians is what it means to be a "spiritual," or "Spirit," people. "Being 'spiritual' in the present [context] means to edify the community in worship (chs. 12-14), because the perfect has not yet come (13:8-13)" (Gordon R. Fee, *God's Empowering Presence* [Peabody, Mass.: Hendrickson, 1994], p. 147). Paul uses a variety of words to describe this, including *charismata* ("a concrete expression of grace"), *pneumatika* ("things of the Spirit" or "Spirit-people") and, in Ephesians 4:7, *dorea* ("a gift"). His use of language to describe spiritual gifts (or Spirit gifts) is ambiguous, and all of Paul's lists are ad hoc rather than definitive.

Questions 1-2. Gordon Fee notes that the Greek word used in verse 1 (*ton pneumatikon*) can be translated either "Spirit people" or "Spiritual gifts" (he favors the former, though most translations choose the latter) (*God's Empowering Presence*, p. 152). In either case the mere fact that an utterance is "inspired" does not mean that a person is being led by the Spirit of God. One remarkable factor in this passage is that these gracious bestowments come from the Triune God: "Spirit," "Lord" (Jesus) and "God" (vv. 4-6). Some study guides try to designate certain gifts as from the "Father" and others as from the "Son" or "Spirit." But all the gifts are from God through the Spirit. Appealing to the Corinthians' pagan past, Paul gives a definitive test for determining the genuineness of the gifts: they will confess Christ as Lord, and they will serve the common good. That, however, does not mean that only confessed Christians may serve God. As Arnold Bittlinger says, "In exercising spiritual gifts we are involved in the restoration (the bringing together again) of God's perfect work in creation. An activity can only be characterized as a spiritual gift when it assists in the restoration of creation, and contributes towards the healing of a sick world. But it will also be true that every such activity and contribution is a gift of the Spirit, even when the individual involved is unconscious of it (cf. Matt 25:27f where the 'gifted' people do not know that they exercised the gift of *diakonia*-service)" (*Gifts and Graces: A Commentary on 1 Corinthians 12-14*, trans. Herbert Klassen [Grand Rapids, Mich.: Eerdmans, 1967], p. 25).

Questions 3-4. In much popular literature on the subject of spiritual gifts several misunderstandings are maintained: (1) spiritual gifts are given at conversion and do not change in one's lifetime; (2) Scripture gives a definitive list of all the possible gifts in 1 Corinthians 12, Ephesians 4:1-16, Romans 12:1-8 and 1 Peter 4:10-11; (3) it is crucial to your spiritual maturity and your own sense of worth in the church that you discover the name of your gift and exercise it; (4) your gift describes your identity ("I am a teacher"); (5) the more spectacular gifts are evidence of advanced spiritual maturity; (6) the emphasis on spiritual gifts threatens the unity of the church and causes schism (Gordon D. Fee and R. Paul Stevens, "Spiritual Gifts," in *The Complete Book of Everyday Christianity,* ed. Robert Banks and R. Paul Stevens [Downers Grove, Ill.: InterVarsity Press, 1997], p. 943).

Paul does not give us a systematic study of spiritual gifts including a definition and an exhaustive list. Rather, he describes the great diversity of the way the Spirit works in the church for the common good (not just our personal satisfaction). Apparently, as we judge from 1 Corinthians 14, the Corinthians were prizing one gift over all the others—the gift of tongues (speaking in an unknown prayer language). Paul's central argument in this passage is noted by his repetition of "diversity" and "to each," "to one" and "to another." *Diversity* includes tongues but not exclusively. The unity of the body is not homogeneous but instead, unity rooted in diversity, like the unity of Father, Son and Spirit. Each member of the body contributes to that rich Trinitarian unity through "gifts," "service" and "workings" of the Spirit (vv. 5-6). Paul is using these words to describe how the Spirit works, rather than to categorize some gifts as "motivation" gifts and others as "service" gifts.

Question 5. Envy of one's brother or sister, or despising the contribution of another member, are both ways of sinning not only against the fellowship but against God, who provides and orders the body as God chooses. Hardly ever does one say out loud, "I can manage without you," but we may think it or unconsciously act that way.

Question 6. On the question of whether some or all of these gifts have ceased since the apostolic age, see study 4, but nothing in the text of the New Testament indicates these gifts were only for the first century.

Drawing on wider Scripture we may describe some of these gifts in the following way:

- "wisdom" (v. 8): not the "deeper things of God" but an understanding of the clear message of Christ crucified as God's true wisdom (see 1 Cor 1:18—2:16) (Fee, *God's Empowering Presence*, p. 166)
- "knowledge" (v. 8): a Spirit utterance that reveals something about God and God's kingdom
- "faith"(v. 9): not merely saving faith but the kind of faith that moves mountains
- "gifts of healing"/"healers" (vv. 9, 28): the gracious working of God through the community or through a person that leads to physical and emotional healing
- "working of miracles"/"workers of miracles" (vv. 10, 28): all kinds of supernatural expressions of power other than physical healing
- "prophecy"/"prophets" (vv. 10, 27): Spirit-empowered speaking that proclaims the Word of God with immediacy and directness to the body of Christ for encouragement and edification (Those who regularly function in this way are called prophets.)
- "distinguishing between spirits" or "discerning spirits" (v. 10): both discerning whether a phenomenon is really from God (1 Jn 4:1) and judging or discerning prophecies, as in 1 Corinthians 14:29
- "various kinds of tongues"/"speak[ers] in various kinds of tongues" (vv. 10, 28): a Spirit-inspired prayer language that is under the control of the speaker but will not be understood by the speaker or others without interpretation

- "interpretation of tongues" (v. 10): a companion gift to tongues (really "languages") that enables the community to understand the heart of the message expressed by the speaker of a prayer language
- "apostles" (v. 27): people who, through the Spirit, plant new churches and break down frontiers for the kingdom of God
- "teachers" (v. 27): those who regularly function with a gift of knowledge and can communicate God's truth so that people learn and apply it
- "helpers" (v. 28): people who serve and care for others in practical ways, such as showing mercy
- "administrators" (v. 28): acts of guidance by which wise counsel is given to the community and those who regularly provide guidance to the community (For "miracles," "healings," "helpful deeds" and "acts of guidance," the original Greek does not suggest the persons who do them [e.g., helpers] but rather the function [e.g., helping], though the English translations smooth out the whole section to read "those who . . .")

Question 8. The "Now or Later" section explores some of the Scriptures emphasizing that it is God and not the members (not even the leaders) who orchestrate the gifts in the body. Each local church is not an accidental collection of saints.

The reference to "desiring the greater gifts" (v. 30) is somewhat puzzling. Many think this means that the gifts mentioned in this chapter are ranked by Paul as more important or less important. But this is completely opposite of Paul's main concern, which is to emphasize the importance of diversity. Even the "less presentable members" receive greater care (vv. 24-25). As we will see in study 4, Paul's concern (which should also be ours) is for what builds up the body of Christ. Tongues with interpretation and prophecy (which is clearly intelligible speech) is of greater benefit to the body of Christ than tongues without interpretation. Paul will take up this matter in chapter 14, but first he wants to express the spirit in which gifts are to be exercised: love.

The "greater gift" cannot be love, since love is a fruit of the Spirit and never called a gift in Scripture. Rather, love is the context in which the gifts should be expressed and therefore is "the most excellent way." Love also demands that we do not contain the expression of spiritual gifts to the gathered life of the body but bring it to all aspects of everyday life in the world.

Question 9. Here are some key facts on spiritual gifts drawn from the research of Robert Clinton: "(1) The Holy Spirit gives all the gifts necessary to accomplish his work in the local church. (2) Each member with his [or her] gift is necessary to the whole body and therefore if any member is not active the body as a whole is weakened. (3) How we exercise our gifts is important as well as the fact that we do exercise it. (4) Each member should have an opportunity to use his [or her] gift interdependently with others. (5) People with leadership gifts are to train others so that every member will contribute to the overall growth of the whole body. (6) God should always receive the credit for our use of gifts whether they be leadership or supportive gifts" (J. Robert Clinton, *Spiritual Gifts* [Camp Hill, Penn.: Horizon, 1985], p. 22).

Study 2. Equipping the Saints for Ministry. Ephesians 4:1-16.

Purpose: To understand how equipping people to use spiritual gifts is not a matter of individual study or training but of life together as the people of God.

Questions 1-2. In the first three chapters Paul sets forth the gospel. We are called first of all to belong to Christ, then to live a certain way and finally to join God in his work on earth. We are called to Someone before we are called to do something. And our life together in the community of Christ is not a mere means to the end of getting God's work done on earth. Unity is the goal. But the thrust of the passage is how the Spirit is the basis of our unity leading to peace (v. 3). The passage is thoroughly trinitarian (Father, Son and Spirit), so that our "given" unity, like a genetic code or an inheritance, is through diversity, as is the very being of the God of love.

But this unity must be maintained, and even attained (v. 13). Gordon Fee says, "The unity that is theirs by virtue of their common experience of the Spirit will be maintained only as the Spirit produces the virtues necessary for it" (*God's Empowering Presence,* p. 700). The result of this Spirit-work is that believers dwell in the bond of peace, which is not mere tranquility but the work of Christ in bringing a halt to the hostility between God and humankind and also between people.

Question 3. There is a marked continuity between the Old Testament and the New on the matter of peoplehood. Under the Old Testament the people of Israel were redeemed, chosen and called by God to be a light to the Gentiles—to bless all the world. As we enter the New Testament we find that once again there is one people, redeemed, chosen and called.

It is more than a matter of technical interest to Bible scholars that the word commonly used for "laity," meaning "second class" and "untrained," is never used by an inspired apostle to describe Christians. And, further, the Greek word from which "clergy" is derived (*kleros*) is used not to describe the distinctive privilege of ordained ministers but to describe how the whole people of God is endowed and appointed by God. In that sense, the New Testament church has no laypersons yet is full of clergy! There is one people, not two. So the two testaments reflect continuity in peoplehood but discontinuity in leadership. In the New Testament there is no equivalent for Moses, the prophets and the Levites—people who uniquely had the Word of God while the rest of the people were bereft. The Spirit has been poured out on all: all are priests; all are bearers of God's Word (prophets); all share the kingly rule of Jesus.

Questions 5-6. David Gordon and a few other biblical scholars hold out for the "clerical" translation of this verse found in the King James Version and the first edition of the Revised Standard Version, namely that God has given apostles, prophets, evangelists and pastor-teachers (these last two roles are intentionally linked) to "equip the saints" (followed by a fatal comma in the English but not in the original Greek) and to *do* the work of the ministry. Gordon argues that (1) the three clauses of verses 11-12 all describe the work of the word *ministers;* (2) equipping is not training; and (3) the work of "ministry" or "service" (they are the same word in the original Greek) refers not to the service rendered by all the saints to God and under God, but to the specialized ministry of the word and sacrament of the ordained ministers. Arguing more widely from the New Testament, Gordon claims, "The distinction between those who labor in preaching and teaching God's Word and those who profit from that labor is a distinction well established by the NT writings themselves"("Equipping Ministry in Ephesians 4?" *JETS* 37, no. 1 [1994]: 75). The "gifted ones" according to this view are not the "saints" (which is always a corporate term and does not refer to the piety of the people but to the fact that the people belong to God); the gifted ones are the apostles, prophets, evangelists and pastor-teachers.

Gordon Fee shows conclusively that such a reading cannot be justified and is a serious distortion of Paul's use of "service" (*diakonia*) in all his letters. Service/ministry is something that belongs to the whole people (*God's Empowering Presence,* p. 707). Pastors are ministers to ministers. Further, the references to apostles and prophets (previously mentioned in 2:20 and 3:5) refer not mainly to offices but to functions, and that apparently of itinerant workers who moved from church to church, as did the evangelists. "Pastor-teachers" seems to refer to settled ministers and leaders of local churches. In contrast with those older commentators (Abbott and others) who argue that the pastor gives the ministry and the saints receive it, P. T. Forsyth cryptically argues that the first duty of the preacher is to teach the church to preach; that is, to equip the saints to bear God's Word in the church and the world. While Paul does not in this passage use the word normally translated "spiritual gifts," the "gifted ones" (implying the gifting of Christ through the Spirit) are the leading Word ministers who serve all the rest of the "gifted ones," empowering and drawing the members of the body into a systemic interdependence and unity under the head, Jesus. No human leader is called the "head" of the church. The leaders are still part of the people ("the saints," or *laos*).

Questions 7-8. The church is a rhythm of gathering and dispersion. The purpose of equipping the saints is not only to build up the body but to bring the glory of Christ and his kingly rule into the entire creation. William Barclay notes how the descent and ascent of Christ means there is no place in the universe that is not subject to Christ (Col 1:16-18), so we do not have a "Christ-deserted, but a Christ-filled world" (quoted in Francis Folkes, *Ephesians,* Tyndale New Testament Commentary [Grand Rapids, Mich.: Eerdmans, 1989], p. 125). The ascension of Christ means he cannot be localized. So instead of "sending" mission teams into the world, we might consider where in God's sovereignty people have already been placed in the work world—in neighborhoods, places of education or political service. A church that interviews and prays for its members in what they are doing Monday to Saturday will soon realize that the main ministry of the saints is in the world. Churches might further reduce, rather than increase, the involvement of people in in-church activities during the week. Some pastors in the time of the Reformation locked the doors on Sunday night and said not to come back until next Sunday.

Question 9. Numbers are significant, but they are not the emphasis here. Rather, it's mutual interdependence, relational integrity, discerning truth from error and ministry at the place of real connection with others (the "joints" or "ligaments").

Question 10. Equipping the saints for ministry in this passage, and in the New Testament generally, is not merely imparting information or developing ministry skills. It is, rather, leading and serving in the body in such a way that the church grows in dependence on the Head (Jesus) and members minister to one another. So the best equipping context is not the theological seminary or Bible school but the local church.

Now or Later. New Testament uses of the word *equip* include the following:
1. The equipper as a *physician* (the classical Greek meaning of "equip," Eph 4:12; 1 Cor 1:10)—reducing a fracture or realigning a dislocated limb; a pastoral ministry as when Barnabas equips Saul (Acts 9:27).
2. The equipper as an *off-duty fisherman* (the secular use of the word "equip," Mt 4:21)—cleaning, mending and folding fishnets to be ready for service; a preparatory ministry as when Titus equips Paul (2 Cor 7:5-6).
3. The equipper as a *stone mason* (used in the Greek translation of Ezra 4:12

for restoring the walls of Jerusalem by lining the stones in their intended place)—a structural ministry, as when Paul tells the spiritual ones in Galatia to restore (equip) someone trapped in sin (Gal 6:1).

4. The equipper as a *potter* (suggesting forming and fashioning clay as in Rom 9:22 and Heb 10:5)—a didactic ministry, as when people are formed in the teaching of God's Word to be equipped for every good work (2 Tim 3:17).

5. The equipper as a parent or a *disciple-maker* (which is essentially an imitation process, as suggested by Jesus in Lk 6:40)—a modeling ministry.

6. The equipper as a *project person* (completing and bringing to perfection, as in 2 Cor 13:9: "our prayer is for your perfection")—putting believers into right relationship with the goal of their faith (the main sense in which "equip" is used in Eph 4:1-16: an orienting ministry).

(These are developed in "Six Ways to Beat the Solo Ministry Trap," chapter seven in R. Paul Stevens, *Liberating the Laity* [InterVarsity Press/Regent Reprints, 1985].)

Study 3. Discovering Spiritual Gifts. Romans 12:1-13; 1 Thessalonians 5:19-22.

Purpose: To explore the practical ways people can become aware of the Spirit's work in their lives.

General note. Paul's letter to the Romans aims at the delicate but practical issue of how the gospel of the "righteousness of God" (1:17) can be worked out in a setting where Jewish Christians are still observing food laws, special days and Torah regulations, and Gentile Christians are not. Chapters 1-11 are devoted to the exposition of the gospel in relation to this, with chapters 9-11 (on the marvelous way that God includes both Jews and Gentiles in his plan of salvation) being the climax of the letter. Now in chapter 12 Paul turns to the practical way the gospel works out in a community composed of both Jews and Gentiles. The whole of his exhortation is based, as he says in 12:1, on "the mercy of God."

Question 2. In many English translations the references to Spirit activities are expressed by the word "spiritual" (something interior to persons) rather than "Spirit-ual" (the work of the Spirit through the person). But in verse 1 the reference to "spiritual worship" (Greek *logiken*) cannot mean "interior," since our whole bodies are involved. Perhaps the word is better translated "sensible" or "making the most sense" (Fee, *God's Empowering Presence,* p. 601).

The Greek world viewed the physical body as a prison for the soul and a hindrance to the spiritual life. The purpose of salvation was to free the immortal soul from the body. The Corinthians were heavily committed to spirituality in this sense, and Paul has to eventually teach them about the resurrection of the body (1 Cor 15). This "living sacrifice" (a kind of oxymoron since most sacrifices involved dead animals) is the presentation of our whole lives, our relationships, our very selves.

Question 3. Self-concept is how we think of ourselves. Self-esteem is how we feel about ourselves. Paul's concern here is not just with self-esteem or self-concept as an act of introspection but with how we function in community life.

Question 4. In harmony with Paul's teaching in Corinthians, Paul here teaches again that diversity is essential to the health of the body of Christ. Interdependence, not independence, is critical to healthy Christian living and ministry. In a sense, the individual Christian—that is, a believer who exists in isolation—does not exist. To be in Christ is to be in Christ's body and to relate to Christ as head.

Question 5. Verses 6-8 are primarily about different ways of serving the church, though each of these may also be a way of serving God and neighbor in the world. In Romans 1:11 the addition of the Greek word for "spiritual" (*pneumatikon*) to "gift" allows for the translation "spiritual gift." Yet, as Gordon Fee shows, "even if *charisma* ('gracious bestowing') does not mean 'gift of the Spirit,' and it does not, the overlap between God's good giftings and the activity of the Spirit is such that Paul would surely have understood all of vv. 6-8 as the working of the Spirit in their community life. . . . For [Paul] they would not be 'Spiritual gifts,' but *gifts of God* which are *effectively brought into the life of the community of the Spirit*" (*God's Empowering Presence*, pp. 606-7, emphasis added).

Notable in the Romans passage is the emphasis not merely on the function of serving (prophecy, teaching, administration, giving aid) but on the attitude and extra dimension of Spirit-empowerment that is given in the act of serving itself. This might suggest that experimentation (going ahead and trying to serve in ways appropriate for your talent and passions) may be one of the best ways to discover whether or not God's Spirit is especially working through you in that way.

A matter of considerable debate is the ambiguous phrase "in proportion to his faith" (v. 6), which has suggested to some commentators that some have a little faith and others a lot of faith. But probably the reference is to faith in Christ and the gospel of the kingdom. This would be especially the case with prophecy (in which connection it is mentioned), as this primary way of speaking the word of God to one another needs to be constantly tested and confirmed by the gospel, as we will see in studying 1 Thessalonians 5:19-22.

Question 6. Some of the English translations of this verse and of a parallel verse in 2 Timothy 1:6 might suggest that spiritual gifts are given by means of a prophetic message (1 Tim 4:14) or through the laying on of hands (2 Tim 1:6). However, the original Greek indicates that spiritual gifts are given "along with" prophetic messages or the laying on of hands, rather than "through the means of" these acts. For example, in Acts 13:1-2, the elders and prophets recognized the Spirit's prior activity and laid hands of commissioning on Paul and Barnabas. The Old Testament background for the laying on of hands is found in Deuteronomy 34:9 and Numbers 27:18-23. While not an exact precedent for ministry ordination, the concern here and in 2 Timothy 1:6 is for the recognition of the community's role in commissioning and of Paul in particular (Gordon Fee, *1 & 2 Timothy, Titus,* Good News Commentary [San Francisco: Harper & Row, 1984], pp. 69-70). No one is to be a self-appointed minister.

Questions 7-9. On the one hand, we are not to put out the flame of the Spirit's work. On the other hand, we are to test manifestations to assure that they are in keeping with the whole of Scripture.

Study 4. Those Controversial Gifts. 1 Corinthians 14:1-33.

Purpose: To explore the value of and conditions for spontaneous Spirit ministry in the church.

General note. My late colleague George Mallone has summarized the arguments for and against the cessation of spiritual gifts after the Scripture was written in the first century. (1) First Corinthians 13:10 says, "When the perfect comes [arguing that "the perfect" is the written Scripture] the imperfect [tongues and prophecy] will pass away" (but this misunderstands "perfect" as the perfect canon rather than the end when Christ comes again). (2) Ephesians 2:20 states that the apostles were eyewitnesses to the resurrection of Jesus and founded the church, and hence the gifts are no longer needed (but this flies in the face of Paul's mention of other "apostles," including the woman Junia, who were not eyewitnesses but served the church in leadership). (3) Revelation 22:18 warns against adding to the book, which, it is claimed, is exactly what prophecy does (but prophecy—speaking directly and immediately—is not to be equated with Scripture, does not add to Scripture and must be tested by Scripture). (4) B. B. Warfield suggests that certain supernatural gifts belonged to one of the three great periods of revelation—the exodus, the time of Elijah and Elisha, and the time of Jesus and the apostles (but while some gifts have lapsed in certain periods of the church through neglect or deliberate rejection, there is evidence from church fathers and historians that these gifts have always been in operation, more or less, and not always by fanatical sects and cults). (5) A dispensational approach to Scripture—the belief that God operates in different ways in different periods and that certain Scriptures are relevant only for a particular dispensation— has led many to say they belong only to the apostolic era (Paul's time) and not to ours. (But how are we to understand Paul's simple instruction to the church then and now: "Now I want you all to speak in tongues, but even more to prophesy" [1 Cor 14:5], and the fulfilled prophecy of Pentecost that old and young, men and women will prophesy and see visions [Acts 2:17-19]?) ("Tidy Doctrine," in George Mallone et al., *Those Controversial Gifts* [Downers Grove, Ill.: InterVarsity Press, 1983], pp. 17-25.)

Questions 1-2. In making the contrast between tongues, where people speak to God but edify themselves, and prophecy, where people edify others, Paul notes that the purpose of prophecy (spontaneous speech from God to the people) is for "strengthening, encouragement and comfort." Contrary to those who argue that prophecy is "adding to Scripture" (though admittedly some have claimed to speak this way), this is the Holy Spirit coming among the people of God as comforter and giving spiritual counsel and help. As noted previously, there is no scriptural warrant in Paul's writing for a "personal prophecy," where someone claims to know secrets about another individual (Fee, *God's Empowering Presence,* p. 170). Prophecy is for building up the fellowship. What Paul is regulating is speech that does not build up others but only builds up the speaker.

Question 3. George Mallone outlines the many fears that inhibit full freedom of Spirit ministry in the church: fear of others (what they may think), fear of ourselves (timidity and distrust of our own motives) and fear of God (like the servant with one talent in Mt 25:25). Other fears include losing friends or relatives, causing controversy, being unbiblical, being changed, succumbing to emotionalism and losing control. These fears can be overcome by faith (Ps 46:1-3; 112:7) (Mallone, "From Fear to Faith," pp. 145-54).

Questions 4-5. Arnold Bittlinger notes: "Paul, of course, is arguing against the use of tongues without interpretation in the assembly, but he affirms that tongues edifies the tongues speaker. There is evidence for this in psychological and psychiatric literature as well as the testimony of tongues-speakers facing extreme hardship or spiritual warfare" (*Gifts and Graces,* pp. 99, 101).

Some Christian groups claim that speaking in tongues is the infallible sign of the Spirit's presence and the certification that a person has been baptized in the Holy Spirit in a second blessing. Speaking to this, Gordon Fee, himself of Pentecostal roots, says, "There is a tendency on the part of some Pentecostals to fall into the Corinthian error, where a 'message in tongues,' interpreted of course, is often seen as the surest evidence of the continuing work of the Spirit in a given community. Paul would scarcely agree with such an assessment. He allows tongues and interpretation; he prefers prophecy" (*First Epistle to the Corinthians*, pp. 659-60).

Questions 6-7. Paul's description of the person who comes into a Christian meeting and cannot say "amen" to what is going on (vv. 16, 23) probably refers to an unbeliever.

According to verse 22, tongues and prophecy can both operate as signs, one negative and the other positive. Tongues are a negative sign for unbelievers, showing God's disapproval and making them aware that they are not in the Way (as illustrated by Paul's quotation of Isaiah 28:11). Prophecy, conversely, is a positive sign for believers since it functions as a sign of God's approval. As Fee says, "Paul's urgency is that the Corinthians cease thinking like children and stop the public use of tongues, since it drives away rather than to lead [the unbeliever] to faith" (*First Epistle to the Corinthians*, pp. 682-83).

Question 8. The reference to communal worship in verse 26 is parallel to Ephesians 5:18-19 and can be compared with the Jerusalem church in Acts 2:46-47. Early Christian worship was (1) participatory, with each person contributing a song, a hymn, a word of encouragement, prayers, a teaching, a vision or a prophecy; (2) Spirit-led, with the Holy Spirit orchestrating the proceeding; (3) creative, with planned elements (such as psalms to be sung) balanced with new songs inspired by the Spirit in one or more members; (4) characterized by joy and thanksgiving.

Question 9. Paul argues that the character of the God one worships is revealed in the quality of one's worship. A God of order and peace is worshiped in an orderly, rather than chaotic, way, and the net result is peace and joy. But peace and order do not necessarily mean somber ritual, and often Paul's plea for diversity of expression and giftedness has been sacrificed for sullen conformity.

Study 5. Spiritual Gifts for Liberation. Isaiah 61:1-9; Luke 4:14-21.

Purpose: To understand how the Spirit's empowerment for service in the kingdom of God leads not only to personal transformation but also to social and cosmic transformation.

Question 1. Three representations of the Messiah are presented in Isaiah: the King (chapters 1-37), the Servant (chapters 38-55) and the Anointed Conqueror (chapters 56-66). "Standing back from the portraits, however, we discover the same features in each, indicative of the fact that they are meant as facets of the one Messianic person" (J. Alec Motyer, *The Prophecy of Isaiah*

[Downers Grove, Ill.: InterVarsity Press, 1993], p. 13). The King, the Servant and the Anointed Conqueror are endowed with the Word and the Spirit, they are concerned with righteousness, and their work embraces equally both Israel and the rest of the nations. In Jesus' baptism the voice from the Father confirmed that he was both the anointed king/conqueror ("this is my son, whom I love," Ps 2:7; Mt 3:17) and the servant ("with him I am well pleased" Is 42:1; Mt 3:17).

Questions 2-3. The "poor" to which good news was to be preached are the downtrodden and the disadvantaged (see Is 11:4; 29:19; 32:7). "Binding up" suggests bringing soothing healing to those suffering from emotional exhaustion or conviction of sin. "Captives" and "prison" suggest both the bondage brought by other people and confinement to a place. Restrictions imposed by people are released and circumstances are changed (Motyer, *Prophecy of Isaiah,* p. 500). "Mourning" covers all the sadnesses and disappointments with life, but there is good reason to think this mourning also includes mourning over sin, as this is the thought of Isaiah 57:18. Instead of ashes of despair put on the head, there will be a crown, a beautiful headdress. The changed clothing on the outside represents a transformed spirit on the inside. They get a new name— Oaks of Righteousness—representing acceptance and status before God.

Question 4. In his classic study of Isaiah, George Adam Smith notes how significant this passage has been for our understanding of the gospel and preaching. "*Good tidings* and the *proclamation* meant so much more than the mere political deliverance of Israel—the fact of their pardon, the tale of the love of their God. His provision for them, and his passion and triumph on their behalf—that it is no wonder that these two words came to be ever after the classical terms for all speech and prophecy from God to man. We actually owe to this time the Greek words of the New Testament for *gospel* and *preaching.* The Greek term, from which we have evangel, evangelist, and evangelize, originally meant good news, but was first employed in a religious sense by the Greek translation of our prophesies" (*The Book of Isaiah* [New York: Harper & Brothers, n.d.], 2:477-78).

Question 6. The references to "favor" and "vengeance" are a dualism expressing salvation as welcome/acceptance and judgment. Significantly, Jesus refrained from quoting the whole text in his one-sentence sermon. His first coming would bring welcome. This would be the "year" of the Lord's favor; his mission was not to condemn the world (Jn 3:17). That "day" would be at his second coming (Jn 5:22-29).

Question 7. In Isaiah 60:7, 10 the Lord's favor is extended to the offering brought by the Gentiles. Now, in Isaiah 61, the year of favor has come. This is

not a picture of a slave state. The aliens and foreigners are now full coopera-
tors in the renewed life of the nation, a window to the New Testament vision
of Jews and Gentiles becoming fellow heirs and members of God's household.
Question 9. Earlier, in Exodus 19:6, God spoke of the whole nation being a
royal priesthood. This had never been realized. But now the prophet foresees
that God's original intention of a priestly people (rather than a representative
priesthood) will be fulfilled. In the further prophecy of Isaiah 66:21 this is
extended to the Gentiles. This anticipates the priesthood of the believing
community in 1 Peter 2:5, 9—a people that represents God's presence and
God's purpose to the world and presents the world to God in intercession.
Originally Adam and Eve were priests of creation. Once again the whole people would be priests of creation and the world. "The wealth of the nations"
being shared with God's people is fulfilled practically both in the offering
Paul collects among the Gentile churches for the poor Jewish saints in Judea
(Rom 15:27) and in the final vision of the nations being brought into the
Holy City in the new heaven and new earth (Rev 21:1-4).

Everlasting joy is the centerpiece of this stunning vision of a transformed
people, society and world (Is 61:7-8). God's gift to his people is an everlasting
covenant (v. 8; see Is 54:10; 55:3). All of this is an expression of God's justice—God's making things right with himself and the world. And God's justice is mediated through the Anointed Conqueror, the Messiah, who is "the
mediator of the blessings of the divine Spirit" (see Is 59:21; Motyer, *Prophecy
of Isaiah*, p. 504).

Now or Later. To know God is to work toward justice and to plead the cause
of the marginalized and oppressed.

The existence of poverty is seen as an evil (Prov 15:15), and the aim of the
law is to eliminate poverty in the land (Deut 15:4). In Leviticus 25 the Jubilee
Year enabled those hopelessly in debt to recover their land. Indeed, Leviticus
25 is behind the great announcement of Jesus in Luke 4:18-19. See also Matthew 25:34-40; Luke 6:20; 16:13-4; James 1:27; 5:1-6.

Study 6. Spiritual Gifts in Relationships. Galatians 5:16-26.
Purpose: To explore how the Holy Spirit empowers people so that their relational life will reflect the qualities of God himself.
General note. This study is important for several reasons. First, the idea that
we can, through a special filling of the Spirit, achieve sinless perfection has a
powerful appeal. Second, while people seldom actually say, "I am holier than
you," many think it, often without recognizing how shoddy their own relationships are. Third, some renewal movements unwittingly set people up for

profound disappointment when they "come down from the mountain." Mostly, though, the study is important because Christians are profoundly troubled that they still have struggles. Indeed, for many, problems only increase when they become a Christian. John Stott says, "We do not deny that there is such a thing as moral conflict in non-Christian people, but we assert that it is fiercer in Christians because they possess two natures—flesh and spirit—in irreconcilable antagonism" (*The Message of Galatians* [Downers Grove, Ill.: InterVarsity Press, 1984], p. 146).

Question 1. Understanding the issues explained in this passage is complicated by Paul's use of *sarx*, usually translated as "flesh" and translated as "the sinful nature" in the NIV. Paul uses *sarx* in differing ways in this letter. Sometimes he is referring simply to something physical (Rom 2:28), such as an illness (Gal 4:13). Other times Paul uses *sarx* where we might say "humanly speaking" or "from a human point of view" (Rom 1:3; 4:1; 9:5). For Paul, the body can be purified, can be presented to God as a living sacrifice (Rom 12:1) and is the temple of the Holy Spirit. But the special way Paul uses *sarx* here has to do with the great enemy of the good life. The "works of the flesh" are not usually physical but personal and emotional; they affect the whole person in relationships. William Barclay says, "The flesh stands for human nature weakened, vitiated, tainted by sin. The flesh is man [*sic*] as he is apart from Jesus Christ and his Spirit" (*Flesh and Spirit: An Examination of Galatians 5:19-23* [London: SCM Press, 1962], p. 22). The way of the flesh (meaning the whole person turned away from God) is contrasted with the way of the Spirit. Significantly, Paul contrasts the *work* of the flesh and the *fruit* of the Spirit: work is something we do; fruit is given.

Verse 17 is not easily understood. Paul is not saying that because of the conflict we are not able to do what we want ("the good I want to do I cannot do") but rather that believers no longer have the privilege of doing whatever they wish; they must now do as the Spirit leads. And the good news is that we are not in a state of helplessness. Indeed, if we walk by the Spirit we "*will not* gratify the desires of the sinful nature" (v. 16, emphasis added).

Question 2. This list is certainly not a list of sins of the body, though the first three are expressed physically. Three of the flesh-works are in the realm of sex: *Immorality* is any unlawful sexual behavior, including sexual intercourse between unmarried persons. *Impurity* is unnatural thinking and moral depravity, the soiled mind that awakens disgust and separates us from God. *Licentiousness* is indecency, open and reckless contempt of propriety. Two of the flesh-works are in the realm of religion: *Idolatry* is the worship of other gods, making images of God or making something one's ultimate concern other than the One who is ultimate. *Sorcery* is secret tampering with the powers of evil through witchcraft or the use of drugs to poison and not to cure. Seven of the flesh-works are in the realm of relationships: *Enmity* is an antagonistic spirit toward others. *Strife* is the outcome of enmity in social relations. *Anger,* or fits of rage, is destructive displeasure or hostility, unlike the anger that is cleansed of self (Eph 4:26). *Selfishness* is orienting our world toward our personal interests. *Dissensions* are disagreements that divide people according to personal, racial or ecclesiastical categories. *Party spirit* involves breaking the Christian community up into cliques. *Envy* or *jealousy* is the pain that springs from another's good. The final flesh-works are manifested in addictions: *Drunkenness* is losing one's self-control through an intoxicating chemical.

Question 4. There are two different ways of understanding the biblical witness about flesh and Spirit: (1) flesh and spirit (note the small *s*) refers to the natural conflict between the lower and higher natures within us—an internal conflict; or (2) flesh and Spirit (note the capital *S*) represents the conflict between pre-Christian (without the Spirit), or non-Christian, life and life in the Spirit. The first is anthropological—having to do with human nature. The second is eschatological—having to do with the conflict of the kingdoms as the Spirit, bringing the new age, counteracts the demands of the old age centered on self and sin. While the first approach may correspond with common Christian experience (that we know what we should do but fail to do it), it does not faithfully render the intent of Paul in Galatians. Further, this "higher and lower nature" approach tends to contribute to the deep-seated conviction that one's bodily life is normally evil.

On the second view, *flesh* denotes humankind in its essence. People do not *have* flesh but *are* flesh (A. C. Thiselton, "Flesh," in *Dictionary of New Testament Theology,* vol. 1., ed. Colin Brown [Grand Rapids, Mich.: Zondervan, 1975], pp. 672-73). Flesh is the whole person turned inward, existing apart from God, in the grip of self-centeredness, finding justification in either licentiousness or legalism (both of which leave us with ourselves in the center). Thus Paul is able to say that if we walk with the Spirit, we *"will not* gratify the desires of the sinful nature" (Gal 5:15, emphasis mine). The flesh has been crucified with Christ (the tense here is a completed action, Gal 5:24). Our challenge, then, is to "live in the Spirit" (note that this is not our higher nature) and to "keep in step with the Spirit" (5:25).

Question 5. Since the Christian life begins with the Spirit, proceeds with the Spirit and ends with the Spirit, we can only assume that living by the flesh can never be the habitual action of a Christian. Flesh-living is either pre-

Christian or non-Christian. Paul gives us absolutely no reason to excuse ourselves in any works of the flesh. The Spirit has been given. The kingdom is already here, though not yet fully come. Gordon Fee comments: "Paul does not hereby suggest that Spirit people never sin. His concern is to describe how vv 13-15 are worked out in the lives of those who no longer live under Torah" (*God's Empowering Presence*, p. 433).

Question 6. The ninefold fruit of the Spirit starts with love, the primary expression of the Spirit's presence and the only way the law will be fulfilled. Love is meeting needs and honoring others with no thought of merit. *Joy* is not only an individual quality but the exhilaration of experiencing God's goodness in community. *Peace* is the wholeness of life that comes through profound reconciliation and completeness, and is, in reality, entering into the presence of God. *Patience* is long-suffering toward those who aggravate us or persecute us. *Kindness* is a disposition that seeks the well-being of others and does not first look at the worst in another person. *Goodness* in words and deeds reflect a life perspective that seeks God's best in every situation and relationship. *Faithfulness* is fidelity and loyalty toward people, covenants and truth. *Gentleness* is the character quality that enables a person to refrain from hurting people, from manipulating or violating the personality of others, and that permits one to yield personal rights for the good of others, a characteristic of Christ (Mt 11:29; 2 Cor 10:1). *Meekness* is not weakness but rather humility. *Self-control* is self-mastery and victory over consuming desires, the ability to live according to one's highest principles.

While we normally read these virtues as individual qualities, they are, in the context of this letter, qualities that will be found in the community of faith as people corporately walk according to the Spirit.

Question 8. The reference to "no law against these" and the parallel, somewhat disjointed reference in verse 18 ("you are not under law") must be understood in the context of the whole letter. Paul is dealing with a community that is being tempted to add Jesus to law-keeping (Torah) as a way of salvation. The Spirit is sufficient for life without Torah, and there is no need to revert to their former life as pagans or, in the case of law-keeping Jews, to accomplish salvation by performance.

Question 9. There is divine-human cooperation in living victoriously. First, Paul insists that life in the Spirit is what enables us to live relationally with God-imaging qualities. But, second, our part is constantly to affirm that our sinful nature has been crucified with Christ. This is not self-crucifixion or mortification of the flesh but full and continuous agreement with God's judgment on our autonomous and self-justifying life. Third, we are to "live by the

Spirit" (5:16) and to "keep in step with the Spirit" (5:25). The move is from the indicative to the imperative; the Spirit leads, and we do the walking (an image derived from a farmer leading cattle or soldiers escorting a prisoner to court). We keep in line with what the Spirit is already doing. Commonly, walking in the Spirit is thought of in terms of guidance, but this is a much larger experience of the Spirit's work in revealing godly character.

Study 7. Spiritual Gifts in the Workplace. Exodus 31:1-11; 35:4-19; 35:30—36:7.
Purpose: To demonstrate how the Holy Spirit is given to believers for their work.

Question 1. The infilling of the Spirit describes three qualities that, added to his natural abilities, suited Bezalel for the work: "skill, ability and knowledge" (NIV). These three qualities in the original language mean (1) "wisdom" (*hochmah*)—to understand and envision what is needed; (2) "discernment"—the talent for solving problems; and (3) "skill"—experienced hands (John Durham, *Exodus*, Word Biblical Commentary, vol. 3 [Waco, Tex.: Word, 1987], p. 409). In the Old Testament, wisdom is not merely information accumulated but practical intelligence for the daily affairs of life. "Skill," the third named attribute, is knowledge gained by experience. Of interest is the fact that Bezalel's name means "in El's [God's] shadow," and Oholiab's name means "my tent is the Father God," a name especially appropriate for one who works on the tent of God (Alan Cole, *Exodus* [Downers Grove, Ill.: InterVarsity Press, 1973], p. 210).

Question 2. Oholiab's ability in working with fabrics is mentioned in the context of "elaborately sewn vestments" or "woven garments" (NIV). This describes braidwork that is stitched and overstitched (Durham, *Exodus,* p. 409).

Question 3. Unquestionably the major context for spiritual gifts in the New Testament is community worship. This is entirely understandable, since the letters of Paul were addressed to congregations. But Paul's teaching about the person and work of the Holy Spirit indicates that the Holy Spirit is given for mutual edification not only in the church but also in the workplace. For many people, work has become an idol, a place to gain their identity and find meaning in life, and the workplace is often characterized by addiction, predatory competition, greed and envy. In situations like this, the sevenfold fruit of the Spirit outlined in Galatians 5:22-23 will transform both worker and workplace.

Questions 4-5. Following the initial instructions for building the tent of meeting, God gives instruction about keeping the sabbath, with additional emphasis on the sabbath as a sign of the covenant relationship between God and God's people. Then follows the terrible sin of worshiping the golden calf. The stone tablets of the Ten Commandments are broken because the covenant is null and void. Moses intercedes on behalf of God's people and prays for the vision of God. New stone tablets are then made, symbolizing the renewal of the covenant, and Moses communes with God on behalf of the people. Then, in chapter 35 the story of the building of the place for the presence of God is recapitulated, this time with the important addition of the teaching gift of Bezalel and Oholiab. These men were to be multipliers.

Question 6. Not only Bezalel and Oholiab but the rest of the craftspeople had a heart to do the work (Ex 36:2 says literally "whose minds prompted them to take on the work and do it"). The women and men brought offerings of gold jewelry, burnished bronze mirrors (38:8), violet and purple (35:6), precious stones, spices and oil (for incense and anointing oil), so much so that Moses had to restrain the people from giving anything more (36:6-67). The volunteerism of the project is everywhere evident. It was "not merely dutiful, it was exuberant."

Question 7. This story illustrates the principle that God leads through the heart, making us want to do the will of God. The thought that "if I want to do it, it cannot be the will of God" denies that we have the mind of Christ, that the new creation is tougher than the old and that God through the Spirit leads us in motivation, often even before we were conscious of God's work in our lives.

Question 8. Before Pentecost the Holy Spirit was bestowed on individuals for special service (Num 24:2; Judg 6:34; 14:6; 1 Sam 10:10; 16:13; 1 Chron 12:18; Ps 51:2). Though the phrase "filled with the Spirit" is used exclusively for Bezalel, other phrases, such as "pouring out" and "resting on," suggest that the Spirit empowered people for extraordinary activities. Paul, however, understood the Spirit as universally given in Christ and as a tangible sign of the end times and coming kingdom of God. Likewise, Peter's sermon on the day of Pentecost, in which he quotes the prophecy of Joel, indicates that because Christ has come, died, risen, ascended and poured out the Spirit, what was once occasional and extraordinary (as in the case of Bezalel and Oholiab) is now universal (Acts 2:17-21).

Study 8. Spiritual Gifts in Witness. Acts 2:1-21, 37-47.

Purpose: To explore how the Holy Spirit equips and motivates the people of God to witness to the good news of the kingdom of God in Jesus.

General note. Before the time of Christ, the Day of Pentecost was celebrated as the anniversary of the giving of the law. In the New Testament, however, it refers to the day when the Spirit wrote the law on people's hearts, fulfilling the promises of the old covenant (Jer 31:31-34). John Stott suggests four ways of considering the meaning of Pentecost: (1) the final act of the saving ministry of Jesus before he comes again; (2) the empowerment of the apostles for the work of planting the church universally; (3) the inauguration of the new era of the Spirit; or (4) the first revival (*Spirit,* p. 61).

Questions 1-3. While the sounds (rushing wind) and sight (tongues of fire) are clearly understood, the question of what actually was said and heard is somewhat ambiguous. Some have argued that there was a miracle of hearing—people from all the known nations of the Roman world heard their mother tongue being spoken, even though the apostles spoke Aramaic or Greek. Others note that the text actually says that they spoke in "other tongues" or "other languages" to the amazement of the gathered peoples who knew these were Galileans, known for being uncultured and having a particular twang in their speech. The latter seems to be the case, though the tongues/languages spoken here may not be the same "tongues" that Paul regulates in 1 Corinthians 14, which apparently were not known languages. Pentecost was a miracle of communication, reversing the curse of Babel (Gen 11:1-9) and empowering the people of God to communicate the wonderful works of God universally, not just to Jews. The church exists in mission.

Question 4. Peter refers to this event as the fulfillment of the prophecy in Joel 2:28-32 that the days of the Messiah and the age of the Spirit have dawned. The kingdom of God has come (though not yet fully), and all the power of the Spirit associated with the time of fulfillment at the end is now here.

Often Christians think that the end times are the time of tribulation and fulfillment just before Christ comes again. And some think the end times are near. But biblically the end times stretch from Pentecost to the second coming of Jesus, a glorious time when all the powers and presence of the new age of the Spirit are present. John Stott notes that the significance of the verb "poured out" illustrates "the generosity of God's gift of the Spirit (neither a drizzle not even a shower but a downpour), its finality (for what has been 'poured out' cannot be gathered again) and its universality (widely distributed among the different groupings of humankind)" (*Spirit,* p. 74). The events of the Day of Pentecost symbolize this. The kingdom of God now transcends race, nation and language, prefiguring the day when there will be a "great multitude that no one can count, from every nation, tribe, people and language, standing before the throne and in front of the Lamb" (Rev 7:9). The continuing quote from Joel about the upheavals in nature may refer to the natural events of Good Friday (darkness and earthquakes), or they may be metaphors of the convulsions of history that are somewhat typical of language used to describe the end times.

Question 5. Significantly, the gifts associated with the last days are those we have previously called the "controversial gifts"—prophecy, dreams and visions, and tongues. Two things are remarkable about this age of fulfillment: (1) all the people in Christ (and not just men and leaders) are so empowered; (2) all the people are given capacity to bear God's Word to others—a universal communication ministry. (See the "Now or Later" section in study 4.)

Questions 6-8. Significantly, it was not the apostles who added people to the church but the Lord (vv. 41, 47). (1) Evangelism is the Spirit's work with which we cooperate. (2) Evangelism involves calling people to repentance and baptism. (3) Evangelism is communicating the "wonderful works of God"—the spoken Word. In the later Jerusalem church it was as "the word of God spread" that "the number of the disciples . . . increased rapidly" (Acts 6:7), a statement repeated in the case of Ephesus (Acts 19:10). (4) Sometimes evangelism is accompanied by supernatural signs and wonders, but sometimes it's not. (5) Ordinary Christians are called to participate in the global, international and interracial expansion of the kingdom of God. (6) Evangelism is not creating isolated believers but adding people to the church. There are no individual Christians.

Question 9. It is often pointed out—rightly so—that this was an emergency situation (thousands stranded in Jerusalem after the feast), and the radical sharing was voluntary. However, the principle of true *koinonia* (sharing) continued even when the believers were scattered, as they were soon forced to do (see Acts 11:27-30; Rom 15:26-27; 2 Cor 8-9).

R. Paul Stevens is the David J. Brown Professor of Marketplace Theology and Leadership at Regent College, Vancouver, British Columbia, and the author of several books on the ministry of the whole people of God and the spirituality of everyday life, including Down-to-Earth Spirituality *(InterVarsity Press). He and his wife, Gail, have three married children and eight grandchildren. Paul loves to canoe, take pictures and make beautiful things with his hands.*